There's No Place Like Home

David Hill

Learning Media

Contents

1. Somewhere Like Earth

Imagine this. Scientists have predicted that, in the year 2020, a huge **meteorite** may hit Earth. It would cause a lot of damage. Dust would block out the sunlight and make Earth too cold and dark to live on. What could we do if this were really going to happen? Could we find somewhere else to live?

*Earth has been hit by meteorites in the past. This **crater** in Arizona was made by a falling meteorite.*

There are eight *other* planets in our **solar system** – maybe one of them is similar to Earth. Could people travel to Venus or Saturn and live there? Let's find out! We need to look for **air**, water, food, solid land, and heat from the Sun. That's what we need to survive.

WHAT IS A DAY?
WHAT IS A YEAR?

A *day* is the time it takes for a planet to spin around once. Earth takes 24 hours. Venus takes over 5,800 hours – that's 243 Earth days!

A *year* is the time it takes for a planet to travel once around the Sun. Planets further from the Sun take longer to make an **orbit**. Mars takes nearly two Earth years to orbit the Sun; Jupiter nearly 12; Saturn over 29.

MERCURY VENUS EARTH MARS

2. The Inner Planets

Earth is one of the four "inner planets," – those closest to the Sun. Let's start by looking at the three other inner planets – Mercury, Venus, and Mars.

MERCURY

Photographs taken by the spacecraft *Mariner 10* show that the surface of Mercury looks a lot like that of our moon, with craters, valleys, and rocky ridges.

Mercury is the closest planet to the Sun. During the day, it's very hot – over 600°F. At night, it's freezing – minus 330°F. That's more than twice as cold as it gets in Antarctica!

How Big Is It?

EARTH

MERCURY

Mercury is much smaller than Earth.

Also, if you camped on Mercury, you'd notice something unusual. Mercury spins only once every 58 Earth days. So from sunrise to sunset takes about 700 hours. Then you'd have 700 hours of freezing night.

Mercury is a dry planet with no **atmosphere**. So ... no air, no water, and unbearable temperatures. You can cross Mercury off your list.

Mercury File

DISTANCE FROM SUN: 36 million miles

DIAMETER: 3,033 miles

LENGTH OF DAY: 58 Earth days

LENGTH OF YEAR: 88 Earth days

ATMOSPHERE: little or none

TEMPERATURE: day: 600°F
night: minus 330°F

MOONS: none

VENUS

Venus is between
Mercury and Earth.
It's about the same
diameter as Earth, and
it's always covered with
clouds. Could that mean water?
No – scientists think that the clouds on
Venus rain **sulfuric acid**!

The clouds also trap in heat, just like a
greenhouse. So Venus is even hotter
than Mercury: over 800°F. That's hot
enough to melt **lead**, so water would
turn to steam anyway. The atmosphere
is **carbon dioxide** gas. Humans need
oxygen in the air they breathe.

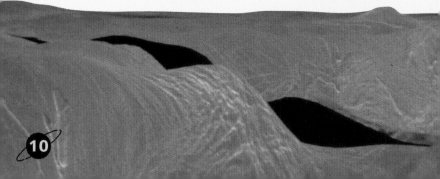

Venus spins backward, so the Sun rises in the west and sets in the east. And it takes 243 Earth days to turn once. Since it takes only 225 days for Venus to orbit the Sun, a Venus day is longer than a Venus year!

How Big Is It?

EARTH

VENUS

Venus is only a little smaller than Earth.

Venus has no oxygen and no water, and it's too hot. Cross it off the list.

Venus File

DISTANCE FROM SUN: 67 million miles

DIAMETER: 7,523 miles

LENGTH OF DAY: 243 Earth days

LENGTH OF YEAR: 225 Earth days

ATMOSPHERE: carbon dioxide

TEMPERATURE: day: 800°F

MOONS: none

MARS

Mars is called the Red Planet because of its rusty-red rocks and dust. It's further from the Sun than Earth is, so it isn't hot – it's *very* cold. If there's any water on Mars, it's probably frozen, deep under the ground.

How Big Is It?

EARTH

MARS

Mars is much smaller than Earth.

There's no air on Mars that you can breathe, just carbon dioxide. Could there be some kind of life on Mars? Scientists hope so, but they haven't found anything yet.

Some day, people might build space bases on Mars, under airtight domes. They might melt the frozen underground water. But at the moment, none of the inner planets (except for Earth) are places where we could live.

Mars File

DISTANCE FROM SUN:	142 million miles
DIAMETER:	4,222 miles
LENGTH OF DAY:	24 hours, 37 mins
LENGTH OF YEAR:	687 Earth days
ATMOSPHERE:	carbon dioxide
TEMPERATURE:	minus 120°F
MOONS:	2

JUPITER   SATURN

3. The Gas Giants

A long way from Mars, past the **asteroid belt**, we find Jupiter and Saturn – the two biggest planets in the solar system. You could fit 750 Earths inside Saturn and 1,000 inside Jupiter. These two planets are called the gas giants because they're made up mostly of **hydrogen** gas. There's no solid land, except maybe at the **core** of each planet.

How Big Are They?

JUPITER

EARTH

SATURN

Jupiter and Saturn are both more than nine times wider than Earth.

15

JUPITER

Although Jupiter is the largest of all the planets, it has the shortest day – less than 10 hours. Because it spins so fast, winds race through its gas clouds at 350 mph.

The Great Red Spot on Jupiter is really a huge storm, twice the size of Earth. It has been raging for the last 300 years.

Jupiter File

DISTANCE FROM SUN: 483.3 million miles

DIAMETER: 88,784 miles

LENGTH OF DAY: 9 hours, 55 mins

LENGTH OF YEAR: 11.9 Earth years

ATMOSPHERE: hydrogen and helium

TEMPERATURE: minus 300°F

MOONS: at least 16

Saturn's rings look solid, but they're made up of billions of bits of ice and dust spinning around the planet.

SATURN

Saturn is as cold and stormy as Jupiter, so you couldn't walk or breathe on it. And there's no water. Cross Jupiter and Saturn off your list, too.

Saturn File

DISTANCE FROM SUN: 886 million miles

DIAMETER: 74,900 miles

LENGTH OF DAY: 10 hours, 39 mins

LENGTH OF YEAR: 29.5 Earth years

ATMOSPHERE: hydrogen and helium

TEMPERATURE: minus 360°F

MOONS: at least 23

URANUS   NEPTUNE   PLUTO

4. The Outer Planets

Scientists haven't known about the outer planets for very long. Pluto was only discovered in 1930. We do know that Uranus, Neptune, and Pluto are so far from the Sun that it would be much too cold there for people to survive.

Uranus and Neptune look greeny-blue, but that's not because of water or plants. The atmospheres of these planets are hydrogen gas. Scientists think they could be like the gas giants, with no solid land at all.

Uranus File

DISTANCE FROM SUN: 1,782 million miles

DIAMETER: 31,770 miles

LENGTH OF DAY: 17 hours, 14 mins

LENGTH OF YEAR: 84 Earth years

ATMOSPHERE: hydrogen, helium, methane

TEMPERATURE: minus 410°F

MOONS: 5

Neptune File

DISTANCE FROM SUN: 2,774 million miles

DIAMETER: 30,757 miles

LENGTH OF DAY: 16 hours, 7 mins

LENGTH OF YEAR: 165 Earth years

ATMOSPHERE: hydrogen, helium, methane

MOONS: 2

How Big Are They?

URANUS   EARTH   NEPTUNE

Uranus and Neptune are both about four times wider than Earth.

What about Pluto? Is it a cool little place? Pluto is certainly cool. It's so far away that no real sunlight reaches it. From Pluto, the Sun would just look like a bright star. The **methane** gas in its atmosphere sometimes freezes onto the planet. It has no air or water.

Pluto takes over 248 Earth years to orbit the Sun. Imagine a birthday once every 248 years!

On the outer planets, there's no air to breathe, no water, and no warmth. Sorry, that's it. Cross the last three planets in the solar system off your list, too.

An illustration of Pluto and its moon, Charon

Pluto File

DISTANCE FROM SUN: 3,672 million miles

DIAMETER: 1,419 miles

LENGTH OF DAY: 6.4 Earth days

LENGTH OF YEAR: 248.5 Earth years

ATMOSPHERE: methane

MOONS: 1

5. The Moons

Earth's moon is mostly freezing cold. It has no air or water.

But there are more than 65 other moons in our solar system. Jupiter has at least 16 moons, and Saturn has at least 18. Maybe one of these moons would be a good place to live? Maybe ... but the moons in our solar system are mostly cold, airless places.

To live on Earth's moon, people would need to take their own supply of air and water.

Io is one of Jupiter's many moons.
Below you can see a volcano erupting on Io.

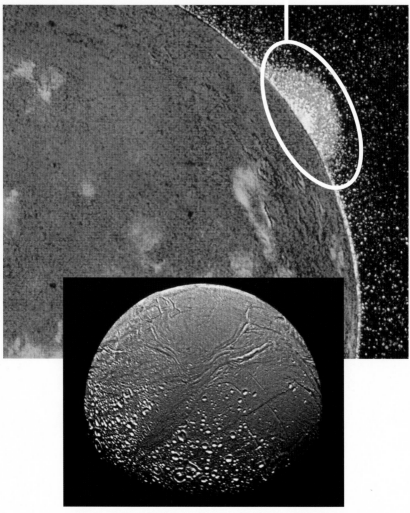

Enceladus is one of the many
moons of Saturn.

However, Saturn has a moon called Titan, and its atmosphere is made of brown gas. A **space probe** called *Cassini* left Earth in 1997 and will reach Saturn in 2004. *Cassini* will drop a small probe onto Titan to test its atmosphere. Maybe Titan could be the future home we're looking for. But you can cross off all of the other moons.

6. The Good News

Don't worry. If a meteorite *was* going to hit Earth in 2020, scientists would still have time to protect our planet. They might send up a rocket that could blow the meteorite apart or change its course.

One thing that we've found by exploring the other planets in our solar system is that Earth is a very special place. We need to protect our planet – the only one in our solar system that has all of the things we need in order to live. There's just no place like our home!

Find out more about the planets.
Visit this amazing website:
www.seds.org/nineplanets.html
You can follow the *Cassini* mission
to Saturn and Titan on:
www.exosci.com/probes/cassini

Glossary

(These words are printed in bold type the first time they appear in the text.)

air: the mixture of gases we breathe on Earth, mostly nitrogen and oxygen

asteroid belt, the: a group of thousands of rocky objects that orbit the Sun between Mars and Jupiter

atmosphere: the layer of gases surrounding a planet

carbon dioxide: a gas found in the atmosphere of some planets

core: the center of a planet

crater: a dent made by an object crashing into the surface of a planet

diameter: the distance from one side of an object to another, measured through the center

hydrogen: an inflammable gas with no color

lead: a soft metal

meteorite: a rock from space that hits a moon or planet

methane: a highly flammable gas with no color or smell

orbit: the path traveled by a planet around the Sun

solar system: our sun and the planets and asteroids that travel around it

space probe: a spacecraft, with no one inside, that explores the solar system and sends data back to Earth

sulfuric acid: a strong, poisonous chemical

Index